Catharsis:
Reflections of Emotions

Thom Love

All rights reserved
Copyright: © 2013 Tom Love
ISBN: 978-1-940359-99-1
Library of Congress Control Number: 2013946469
Burkhart Books, Bedford, TX 2013

All rights reserved as permitted under the U. S. Copyright Act of 1976
No part of this publication may be reproduced, distributed,
or transmitted in any form or by any means, or stored in a database
or retrieval system, without the expressed written permission
of the author and publisher.

Cover photo by J Thom Love
Cover devloped by Amanda Grace Butt

BurkhartBooks

Bedford, TX
www.burkhartbooks.com

In Memory of

Lynda

daughter,

    sister,

        wife,

            mother

For

    Our

        Children

Contents

In Memory of Lynda	3
Introduction	9
Words—	19
Butterfly Wings	21
Sayings	23
Fate	25
Nothingness	27
Friendship	29
Snow	31
Premise	33
The Child is Born	37
A Surgeon's Prayer	39
San Francisco Glimpses	43
Streams of My Youth	49
Depression	57
Life	59
Texas Evening	69
Leaving	73
Goodbye Dallas	77
The Beach	81
Sandollar	85
There was a tree	87
Christmastide	91
Nostalgia	95
Life is so short	99

Evening tired	101
I love the sound of your voice	103
Remembrance of a March Day	105
January	110
It is not death	115
My Footsteps	117
I watch you from day	121
I have watched you fall.	123
We deny a lot on the	125
The fear I have most	127
The time is here	129
I bury myself in	130
I do not feel bitter	131
Touch me	133
I do not believe	134
October	137
How important is Touch!	139
Who can understand?	141
The agony I feel	142
I will love you forever	143
December 22	145
On and on this	149
An Afterthought	151
January 2nd	152
I believe	158
After Winter Must Come Spring!	161
February	162
It is over!	163
There is a small corner	164

In the bleakest winter of	166
I reached out my hand	168
Sweet agony	169
People are but the	170
You Are Gone	171
I think of you now	173
It is the time of year	175
I walked today	178
Life is a Gift	180
Am I as the child soul	182
Dreams	185
A falcon lit upon my shoulder	186
To hope and dream	188
Apathy	189
Wait for me there—	192
The Marsh	194
Truth is as variable as perception	200
I walked the grassy of the Llano uplift among	203
Lessons Learned	206
About the Author	209

Introduction

Growing up in the Piedmont region of North Carolina; rich in Scottish, (Scotch-Irish) heritage, I was a romantic from an early age. Marrying my high school sweetheart in our junior year of college was viewed with skepticism by many. With little but hope and confidence, she taught school while I began medical school. For financial considerations, I took the US Navy senior medical program, which obligated me to several years of service. Two years at the Naval Aerospace Medical Institute in Pensacola, Florida, was followed by a year in Vietnam. While there, I began writing. Encourage by others at home, I continued to write after returning from Southeast Asia and during my training in Dallas at Parkland Hospital.

During our time in Dallas, Lynda, my first wife, began having premonitions that she had some serious illness, even expressing to friends that she did not believe we would grow old together. Busy with training and with little time for home life, this notion of impending illness seemed extremely unlikely to me. After completing the four-year residency program, an opportunity to go to Korea to work at a church-sponsored hospital became available. This had been planned in the past, and was considered as a temporary move for only one or two years. For the first time in our relationship, Lynda resisted, stating, "What will we do if I should need hospital and medical care?" This did get my attention. Instead of going to Korea, I joined the teaching staff at the University of Texas in Galveston, Texas. Within six months, we knew she did indeed have incurable and inoperable liver cancer.

The following year was six months of tolerated treatments, followed by six months of fluctuating hope and despair. I voiced all of these emotions by continuing to write. She lived a year when life expectancy was two to six months, I believe she lingered because of our children, who were then thirteen, ten and six years of age. Lynda died on January 2nd because, [she said,] "I do not want to die on a holiday and have good times marred by bad memories."

With her illness and death so consuming for all the family, I believed I could no longer effectively treat nor counsel cancer patients. My emotions were always too exposed, and my desire was to console, touch and advise patients and family candidly "what you are really facing." Rather than repulsing most patients with my candor, I was often sought out.

Looking back, there were four distinct events that one could perceive as helping prepare me for this personal loss.

As a senior in medical school, my mother, who was always involved in the lives of others, told me (not asked) to go visit a minister she knew whose son was in the university hospital with a brain tumor. I always semi-resented my mother's insistence to include me in her ideas of neighborly intrusion into the lives of others, but I usually complied. So I met this stranger late one evening. We talked for hours.

His nine-year-old son was dying of an inoperable brain tumor. The onset of his illness was subtle; just a slight limp and stumble that gradually became undeniable, resulting in the diagnosis being made. This disease for a nine-year-old was bad enough, but what stayed in my mind was the agony of the father. "All my career I truly believed I provided comfort and guidance for my parishioners during illnesses, loss, stress and grief," he told me. "I now know that all my euphemisms, all the platitudes designed to comfort were useless. I now know that no words, no effort to console can begin to reach the depth of my grief. All my efforts, while honest and sincere, were in vain," he said.

From that encounter until today I have tried to avoid any words that may tend to invalidate or minimize grief or loss—including my own.

While interning, my call schedule was every other night in the hospital, which meant that, in order to have a weekend off from Saturday noon until Monday morning, one had to stay within the hospital Thursday and Friday until noon on Saturday. There was a 36 year-old lady whom I met by accident. She was being treated as an in-patient for breast cancer. I enjoyed going by her room while on call to talk about trivia. One Saturday morning when anxious to go home for the weekend, we talked longer than usual. She spoke of her five-year-old daughter and how she was unafraid of dying, but how much she worried about leaving her young daughter. She talked of how she was grieving over the unfinished task of raising the child into adulthood and all the things she would miss. Then she bluntly stated, "I am now dying, and much too soon." I could offer no insight nor help, for I was not even aware of the specifics of her medical condition. I left for my weekend unnerved by her adamant declaration of impending death as well as being somewhat guilty for my hurrying to go home. Monday, after required work, I hurried to her room to relieve my uneasiness only to find an empty bed. When asked, the floor nurse confirmed that she, the woman with breast cancer, had died the night of our conversation. "She was a nice lady," the nurse calmly stated. "She left you a present." The nurse handed me a wrapped package. Opened, I held an afghan she had knitted for my daughter, who still has this remarkable gift. I never again would question nor trivialize one's perception of his or her own mortality.

Heath was a doctor in training friend of mine who was held back for one year as an intern after he and his wife were hit head-on by a drunk driver on their way to Virginia Beach. He was mildly injured, but his wife sustained massive head trauma that left her alive with no cerebral functions. I talked to him about his difficulties pertaining to his marriage and life. His wife's parents blamed him, never accepted the prognosis, and never visited their daughter, who was then in a full care facility. His visits to see his wife were initially daily until total lack of recognition and cognition gradually resulted in diminishing visits. After months he was able to begin to think of the future. I remember him telling me, "I'll always love my wife, but she is no longer in the body that is in the bed. I will always care for her and be responsible for her care, but I know that I must go forward with my life rather than involute with her. So the day may come when I may have to divorce her, still remaining her guardian for as long as she lives."

Little did I know that I, too, would be blamed for events beyond my control and that my wife's parents would not come to see their daughter during her last year.

Years after Lynda's death, I planned to attend a seminar on Native American spirituality within the Four Corners region of the United States. Two weeks prior to the meeting a nephew of the leader came to my home to return the prepaid fees. Confused, the nephew explained to me that his uncle had recently been diagnosed with an inoperable esophageal cancer and that he was taking this time to go for a healing. Hesitantly I responded that from what was described the healing would unlikely cure the disease. "Oh no," replied the nephew, "a healing is not for a cure but for acceptance." "Ah yes," I replied, for I understood well, as I had yet to fully accept my loss.

It is hoped that this one man's journey through loss, anger, grief, mistakes, guilt and, finally, acceptance may somehow help others. This is not intended to be a primer to be followed, but as a help to understand ourselves and others. I made many mistakes as well as some good choices. Perhaps the greatest lesson is to learn to forgive ourselves, that we may truly understand and forgive others.

Catharsis:
Reflections of Emotions

Just back from Vietnam, Lynda and I met POW wives who were having great difficulty because our government discouraged any public acknowledgment of their plight. A central location, our home became a meeting place where these women met, talked, and boxed the allowed shipments to their husbands, if alive. I collected soap, toothpaste, brushes, etc., which had been donated by pharmacies in the area. Within two years this movement became nationally active and finally recognized by our leaders.

Although no longer meeting in our home, Lynda especially remained close with these women. She stayed up late the night of the POW's return home. Of the 28 from the Dallas-Ft. Worth area, only four returned home. We went and bought four bottles of champagne, and I wrote the notes to attach to the bottles.

Words—

Inadequate to express,
    Thoughts and feelings
    So important,
Yet difficult to share.
Let us speak little.
Rather—
    Hold my hand and feel my heart,
    Look into my eyes
        and read my soul,
        for I am simple there.

Our home in Dallas was typical of tract development homes with low-end appliances. The dishwasher broke many times, but usually I could fix the problem. We could not afford a new dishwasher. Once when I arrived home on Saturday after two days in the hospital, I was once again greeted with the news of the non-functional washer. In disgust I kicked the miserable machine. Having struggled for days with the dishwasher, Lynda began to cry, in part because she hated to once again present me a problem. I felt terrible, but once said or done, such deeds cannot be retracted.

Butterfly Wings

I have learned with pain
    That the soft velvet beauty
        Of butterfly wings
Can be crushed as easily
    With the careless touch
        Of sincere love
As with a bold fist.

Much of the thoughts along these lines were derived from my experiences with the Marine Corps in Vietnam. Even the one about gifts was from the Oriental philosophy of giving and receiving.

Sayings

The price of security is mediocrity.

Rules are made to keep idiots out of trouble
And for wise men to interpret.

One of the best gifts to give
another is to receive,
gracefully allowing the
other to give.

Richard Parker Anderson grew up in the same area of North Carolina as I. We became friends, fraternity brothers at college, and later he was an usher at my wedding. After college he joined the Marine Corps and became an aviator, while I went to medical school. After serving in Vietnam he returned home to become a Braniff Airlines pilot while remaining in the Marine Reserves in Dallas, Texas.

After my training I, too, went into aviation as a flight surgeon, serving in Vietnam with the Marines. Returning home, Dallas Naval Air Station became my exit billet. At this point in time we had not seen each other for eight years, and I was anxious to see him again after such a long period.

One Saturday, less than a month home and on call at the air base, we had an alert of a crash of a jet fighter. The corpsmen brought the pilot into the first aid area where I pronounced the death of my friend.

Fate

Fate is the breath of life
    That brushes our cheeks,
    Making us aware of the intangible
    forces touching our lives
As the movement of branches
    Gives credence to the wind.

For my yearly two-weeks of Naval Reserve duty, I rode a destroyer from Spain to Charleston, South Carolina. During the transit, the ship crossed the edges of two hurricanes in extremely rough waters. Between rough seas, the water became glass smooth.

Nothingness

The vastness
    Of nothingness
Awes me
Like mid-ocean
    On a glassy day,
When the horizon
Seems to fuse the sea and sky,
Yet just beyond
    My awareness
I know
    Teems vibrant life.

Friendship

The joy
    Of recognizing a friend from afar
    Before distant features
        Can be assured
            And all that is certain is
        The warm glow.
That is what friendship is—
    Joy...
        The warm glow
        Indifferent to distant
            Unimportant features.

January, and it is cold in Dallas. I am returning home for the weekend after more than 48 hours of duty at Parkland Hospital when it began to snow huge flakes that seem to float languidly in the unusually still air. Taking a back road home, there is no traffic and I stopped by the railroad tracks to enjoy the moment. Out in the open among the slowly tumbling flakes, I feel like I am in a large soundproof room where the silence seems deafening and enchanting.

Snow

White lightness
    Floats like a million
        butterflies,
An infinity of pattern
    To caress the earth
        And flutter in the
        slightest breeze,
            While crunching
                beneath my feet.
A wonderment!
    For such active, beautiful
        light things
Should be warm.

We joined a local church that had a young adult class taught by a former minister. He was a wonderful teacher, but I believed he had significant doubt and worry about his own mortality. Having recently returned from Vietnam, where I, too, had to face these questions, I tried to express some of my own beliefs.

I did not think this was well received.

Premise

The audacity of this earth
  To slowly turn
    And set her sun
    On my day!
How inconvenient of this body
  To grow tired and old
    Before this loving task
    Of living is over!
Yet how lovely—
  How appropriate
    Is the sunset
    That proclaims rest
    With the thrill of the unknown.
The day, it seems,
  Is too short—

Although the hours at times drag—
    For me to finish all I desire,
    And I cling to each moment
        With a passion for life
        [and accomplishment]
        Until I, too, must sleep.
God, fill me with awareness
    Of this allotted time.
        Make me self-honest
    So I may meet each person
        With a new love.
In this way, perhaps I can
    Also love myself,
        the ultimate
        In growth and maturity
           That one can obtain
        By the end of our day.

Some friends adopted a child, which I thought was wonderful. This was perhaps a misguided effort, in that this was also questionably received. The thought and effort was honest.

The Child is Born

The child is born.
The parent is made in
The rocking chair
Ever watchful and hopeful
Of equal or better life.
Lasting love, too, grows from hardship
While respecting and fulfilling
Those special needs of another,
Receiving honestly, revealing weakness
Becomes as crucial as strongly
   giving—
The wonderful paradox of receiving.
Yet giving by allowing the other
To be needed.
So in life as in birth,
Only the child is born.
Love ensues through
Caring and giving.

My mentor, C. Culbertson, was an excellent teacher by example. Some were deterred by his religious beliefs. I was not because he lived his belief. I wrote this for him. It was well received.

A Surgeon's Prayer

God give me wisdom
    So I may remember
        That at my best
            I remain fallible
Unable to heal a wound,
    Cure the sick,
    Create with surgery
    Anything that can match
        The original design
        Or save a life
Grant me judgment
    More than proficiency
        That I may know my
    limitations
    Diagnose well to best choose
    treatment

Recognize surgery as essential only
For the lack of available cure,
And prolong life whenever I can
While respecting the dignity of
dying
Bless my hands
That I may achieve these hopes
And become a credit to the greater
Plan and receive my main reward
Of the smile of gratitude and a
Sincere belief that even in failure,
I have done my best.

I had a two week Naval Reserve duty at Oakland Naval Hospital. A large, undeveloped hill was immediately behind the hospital, and I took some leisure time to climb this hill in solitude.

San Francisco Glimpses

I followed the trail
   Through the grass
      Now bent heavy with golden seed
      Rippling in the bay breeze
I followed the deer to the top of my hill
   Which I alone now possess
      While watching the
         hawk & dove
      Fly their patterns in the sky
I lie here now exhausted
   And sink into the grass
      That rattles seeds' heads
      As each stalk bends to push
         The chill bay wind

off my face
And the sun glares down
In warm profusion
Now peeking through a
rising mist
That hides the cities,
[their bridges and water,]
Then rising as rushing clouds
Over my head
From this rocky bed
With the summit beneath my head,
I watch the centipede
Of the vibrant freeways
In its lemmings rush
To where?
Always confined to the highways
Never to venture
To places as my perch

Where one can watch
    From afar—and ponder
      Where man goes
        On such limited
          roads.
But this is paradoxical
    San Francisco
Intimate with the wild, cold sea
    Yet lofty with the mountains
    Where highways and
streets cannot hide the Monet
    Of colors in the discordant
      growth of flowers
    Among the hills of green
    With soft brush strokes
      How inconsistent the area
    As barren, scrubby hills suddenly
yield

    To valleys of redwood giants
    And sandy beaches that spring
    To the rocky westward precipices
People
    The mundane,
    the sophisticates,
    The profane,
    and those who try
        To be another
    Walk in peace —
    Each to the cadence of his
        Own drum
Whatever one seeks
    He can find
        For San Francisco is
        where
        The hawk and the dove
            Can fly their own

patterns
In the sky
And never duel.

Having finished my training, I began to realize that I had followed my hopes and dreams to specialize myself into a lifestyle far different from my youth—into one I did not like?

Streams of My Youth

I want to return to the streams of
    my youth
    Sit on the bank
        Dangle my feet in the coolness
        Watch the footprints
        of the wind
        Across the wet
            smoothness
            And ponder again –
How many raindrops make a
    cloudburst?
How many blades turn a brown valley
    green?

How many petals turn green into
    sheens
        of blue and red?
How much sky does it take to make
    blue?
How does wind blown mist make
    dynamic whiteness?
Why does smooth, warm skin feel so
    good?
Or why does revealing oneself to a
    friend warm the soul?
I have wandered far,
    Worked and dreamed of
    structured goals
    Into a funnel's neck,
        realizing most
        until now,
    When those so-important

*yearnings
seem trite compared with
the simple aspirations of youth.
Is it compromise
Or growing older
That makes me want to turn
around
In this maze
To the self-honesty and
simplicity
Of dangling my feet again
In the streams of my
youth?*

For those who have never seen Texas Hill Country springtime, there is an unbelievable bloom of wildflowers that is an absolute marvel. The spectical is worth a trip from far away.

My Field

They cut down my field—
    The one I pass each morning
    To Face the sameness f each day
They mowed my field
    which faced each
    morning sun
    with pert dots of orange, yellow,
blue and pink
like mirrors of colored life.
Dots of asymmetry, fusing in numbers
    on a velvet of green
    Stretch beyond the distant trees
    As to infinity—
Testimony to the total harmony of

nature.
How this field made me feel good and
	fresh!
	In this land of black scarring
		roads,
	Poles, lines and signs.
I wonder—
	Did the man on the tractor know
	He was destroying a master
		piece?
Someone destroyed my field—
	Until next spring—
	I hope.

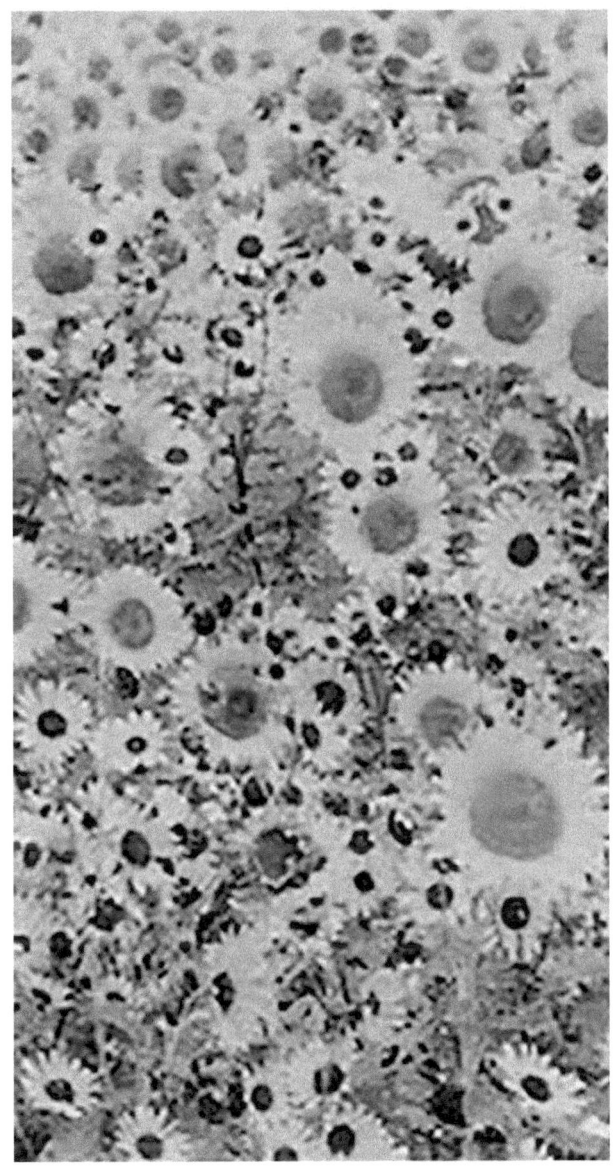

Depression

Some days, as today,
   I seem to walk the tight
     Between up
       and
           down
And blue-grey shadows
   Seem to cling to my heels
A ghost lurks,
   Unreal
     Yet present
Ready in my thoughts
   To bound forward
     And command my
       spirit
It is on days as today

That solitude and music
Can lift the veil
And change the
uneasiness
Into productive
warmth.

Life

God:
    I love this life
    These colors, this air, this flesh
        The very weakness that
            limits me.
I want to love this world
    With a naked unabashedness
        Equal only to the innocence
    Of a new born child
        And feel unashamed
    in the freedom
I want to feel the beauty
    In all the mucus and slime
        That I can digest
            And suck all the succulence

This world can offer.
Who am I, God
   But the tendons, blood, and sweat
      You created?
What is foul
   Except that which I have
      been taught?
If God be
   May I see His image
      In the lowest
If Christ be
   May I find all men His mirror
If there be heaven and hell
   Should I look further than
      his life?
         For I have lived and tasted
            Bitterness equal to hell
            And enough sweetness

To be of heaven
Within this one,
wonderful
Life
experience.
If there need be morality,
May I never, knowingly or
willingly,
Harm or exploit another
living
Soul

God –
I want so to live,
Feel, Taste, Hear, Smell
and See
All this life can offer with
an ardor that radiates
Love of life and mankind

With each heartbeat
Until that thin mucoid thread is also
Broken,
    Exhausted only from the
        pursuit of living.

Daughter

A daughter is
    As the spring's butterfly
        Lite, bouncy and gay
        A study in soft, delicate beauty
Those who guide her
    Must strive to encourage
        The strength and character
            Sufficient to survive
                The reality of summer
And yet preserve
    The soft, sweet colors
        Of spring

Separation

What am I to you
  I ponder this night
  Since miles apart
  I cannot look into your eyes
  To feel your heart.
Yet with words
  That feel sincere
  We touch—
  The special touch
This aura humans have!
  This boundless vibrance
  That can skip the miles—
  Yet lacking by some—
  Although skin does not touch.

What am I to you?
  I am what you will
  As long as you will.

Texas Evening

The lone whippoorwill sings
  A memory from my past
    of moonlit nights
    Breeze, clear & warm,
    And the evening star,
      First among thousands
      That soon appear
        as grains of silver.
The trees, once fluffy green
  Merge into each other
  Losing identity and seem to me
  As puffs of velvet violet.
Frogs sing their chorus
  Amid the chatter of insects
  And cries of birds
  As if they, too seek

Company in the after-light
The owl tops the evening
  And seems to say—
God is in His heaven
  Peace abounds on this—
    My earth
Hold my hand,
  Let us feel together
This life
    This spring evening in Texas

Leaving good friends in Dallas was difficult, but we knew that our four year stay was to be a way station to a more settled life. So leaving was a mixed emotional experience—not desiring to leave friends, but anxious to move on with our new life.

This was Lynda's favorite...

Leaving

Do not look into my eyes
   And say how much you hate for me
to go
  We know mutual loss
    But possession stiffles
    And respect soon dies
Rather—
  What have we been
    I to you
    And you to me?
We have given and received
  The greatest gift
  Given to another—
    Ourselves—as we are,
    Absorbing from the other

Those infinite, indefinable
 Tidbits of character
 Often not even recognized
 by the owner.
So, I have assimilated a
portion of you—
 Your gifts to me
 Into my being.
Wherever I go
 A little of you will be
Whomever I laugh
 Your smile will be there.
Whenever I touch
 You will touch
When I have feeling
 That unique, sensitive, soul
 of the individual—you—
 Will, also be alive.

If there is immortality,
 Surely, it lies—in part—
 Within the human spirit
 When honestly given and
  shared,
 Assimilated forever
 Within all we touch.
You are,
 Forever a part of my being.

We accepted a teaching position at the medical school in Galveston, Texas. The move was exciting and we greatly looked forward to a new start.

However, driving onto the island, one was met with less than beautiful byways and buildings.

Goodbye Dallas

Goodbye Dallas!
  I have known you well
  For what you are—
  The shining glass buildings,
  Rapid and full freeways.
    And the violence
    Among the throngs.
I disliked my first impressions,
  And still do.
But I know myself better now
  And accept easier
    first feelings that later
    change—
  for beneath the orderly,
    sterile

Construction units lies
   The heart of the city—
    Its people
And I now hate to leave this
  My city
Yet the highest adventure awaits
  for more people are there to meet
  And I must grow.
Hello Galveston
  I do like my first impressions!

Galveston beaches are nearly free of tourists in the fall and winter, , leaving the sand and surf to individuals. Such times can be magical for those who at times have to brave the elements for solitude.

The Beach

This is my island on this earth
  Separate from the throngs
  Yet conjugal with nature
  Where I can voice my throes
    To the soft indifference of the wind.
This crescent of sand is mine alone
  For the moment
  With its backdrop of bleak, stoic rock,
  Lights of radiant blueness,
  Audience of clapping waves
  And dancing of graceful birds
  That race the fingers of the sea
    Upon the defiant shore.
Here I can open my soul,
  Bare myself of the shackels of worry,

Lull myself with the
   primordial rhythm
   of the waves
   And become again the simple child
   Of the universe
   Whom I truly am.
Who am I?
   Where do I go?
   What is the essence of this life I
cherish?
   Questions that seem to echo
      with each roar,
   Rush and sizzle of each wave.
These thoughts, too general
   for the plan
   Of the day—
   I can examine while
      allowing my body

To be carressed by the sand
 and water,
 With all the saltiness of
  life and death.
How sensual!
 How simple!
  How refreshing to the soul!

During this fall, I greatly enjoyed all aspects of walking the beaches, picking up shells and looking within myself.

At this point, I had no idea what lay ahead in the near future.

Sandollar

A captured shadow
　Of a life that was.
　Only silica
　　With protein for glue.
The sandollar
　Lies in the beach wash
　　Waiting to be pulverized
　　Into the simple grain from
　　　Whicn it came,
　　Or to be held and beheld
　　　As a study
　　　　Of the strength of fragility,
　　　The symmetry with asymmetry.
The charisma of holding
　The captured shadow
　　Of a life that was!

There was a tree

That shaded the early
  summers of my youth
And its abundant greeness
  Grew within the sky
About its base
  Massive roots gnarled the
   ground
  Making tunnels to hide
   my treasures
And waves upon an ocean
  of green grass
Patches of blue violets
  Floated upon this sea as if
  tossed by the wind.
I would spend hours looking up
  Into the blue
   Filled with umbrellas of green

And down
  Into the green
    Filled with tufts of blue.
Green in blue—
  Blue upon green
  Blue holding the green
  Green yielding to blue.
It takes much time and growth
  To accept the gift of
    inward sight
  Realizing not all have such sight
  Nor ever care to see
  The beauty ad mystique
  Of blue on green—
    Green within blue.

For the first time in my marriage, my very competent and efficient wife could not muster the energy to buy not write Christmas cards. This was the beginning of my recognition that something was significantly wrong, although there was no obvious or glaring health problems.

I wrote this as a letter and sent copies to all our friends—the realization of serious problems would soon come.

Christmastide

Beyond the tinsel, gifts
  And the bustle
  To do the expected rituals.
Beyond the forevers
  That comprise our lives
  And the evergreen with berries,
Beyond the beliefs
  Of the perfect birth
  And the Christ,
Rests the essence
  Of the celebration
  And the birth.
Christmas of quiet
  Recounting of who we are

And that which is essential
To our lives
Fills my thoughts.
What evolves is a wish
For everyone to give and
receive
The true gift of love —
This card is but a touch —
An effort to pause and say
Friends are and shall
remain
The most important facet
Of our lives
And offer a wish for peace
And a Merry Christmas for all.

A trip home to North Carolina and walks along Duke University's gardens and walkways made me very nostalgic. I think the degree of nostalgia was enhanced by the realization of growing older and that I cannot go back to former lives and times.

Nostalgia

Why do steps seem hollow here
  Where I walked and
    laughed before?
Were not these very blades of
  grass there then
  When our lives, as
    remembered, were so happy?
I feel haunted
  For the dog barks are different
  And the children's play sounds
  Echo too much amid the buildings.
The buildings!
  They were here then, too,
  And the sun, rain, sea-waves,
  This very air I breathe —
  All were here.

Where are my friends—
  What are their names?
  Do even these escape my grasps
    Upon my past?
Around me swirls they,
  Whose lives belong to the now.
  As if mocking my claim to memory.
Memory—
  Why should I linger
  Within this glow
  While my life spoils
  Clinging to my treasures of the mind.
A pause for nostalgia
  Is good only to teach us
  That which should be
    savored
  In the now,
  Earned in the future.

Perhaps at this junction of our lives, I somehow realized that our lives, together, would be short. She had already expressed this belief.

Life is so short
So insignificant
In view of total time
And the universe.
That significance
Can be obtained
Solely through
Our interactions
With
Others.

Much more than sensual, joint showers provided quiet time to discuss family matters and issues as well as time of reaffirmation of caring.

Evening tired
And I love my shower
hot—
Yours is more warm.
When we shower
It is some where between.

I routinely called home for no other reason that to feel grounded. She never complained of having her day interrupted by no specific reason.

I love the sound of your voice

It is warm,

Soothing

And makes me feel good.

Like your touch —

Vibrations of the

inner self.

March still has cold days that are usually windy. Beaches are usually deserted and perfect for solitude.

Remembrance of a March Day

I love days as today
  When the wind blows strong
  Out of the north
  Yet, the waves continue to
    push beachward
  From the south.
These forces meet over the second bar
  With the waves cresting,
  Pushing onward—
  Yet the wind—
  It blows steady
  Catching each wave before the curl,
  Nebulizing the plume and
  Flinging the spray

Gulfward.
From my view
 The illusion is of a great
 Herd of stallions
 Racing in orderly legions to my shore
 With their great white manes
 Rippling in the wind
 To their feathery tips.

We went to the beach to fly kites with our children when she told me to take her a chair as she could no longer walk far. Startled by this statement, I took a chair and was indeed alarmed that she could not walk twenty feet. The next work day, I approached an internet friend and tried to explain my worries. But there were not concrete signs—only symptoms of weakness. After explaining that my wife was not only extremely competent, but normally energetic, he agreed to place her in the hospital for some tests.

Resting in the hospital, she looked as a poster child for good health. Only X-rays determined lesions of the liver. After eleven days in the hospital and with evidence of liver tumors, I persuaded a friend to perform exploratory surgery on a Saturday morning. A general surgeon volunteered to be my envoy in the operating room to keep me informed.

The night prior to the surgery, I was restless and had difficulty going to sleep. When I was able to sleep, I had a disturbing dream that I was a reluctant passenger on a small plane with an arrogant pilot.

We took off overloaded in a fog to enter a circle of tall trees with no exit. I awoke with a start to realize that I overslept. Rushing to the hospital, no nurse would look at me, my envoy absent. I then knew that the news was worse than bad.

Another friend rode me to the beach where I walked and cursed the wind and hid my tears in the salty spray.

January

A north wind blows, chilling the air,
  Meeting the moist warmth
    of the Gulf
    Over the island,
  The fog of winter forms.
My heart, too, was chilled today
  And a fog grips my soul.
  Each defiant struggle sears
      my being
    A little more—a little more!
  Raw and sensitive I stand
  Unable to hide from the
    suffocating plume.
Night-time and I cry—
  Out of desperate despair

And an emptiness felt in my soul
I cry the universal sound of
   hopelessness
I cry in my shower
Yet the tears still loudly fall
In cadence with my pulsating
Fear of loneliness that surges
   Then falls—
   But ever present to rise again.
Oh, God!
 How defiant I have stood
 Knowing my limits,
   I believed,
   Feeling my strengths,
     nurturing pride.
 And yet here I stand
   Unable to bear this pain.
How could I forget in my

quest for life
That being—
  My strength of being
  The fulcrum of my defiance
   Essence of my living, my love,
My wife.
Would that it could be
  I had wound I could see,
  Pain I alone could bear,
  Hurt I could blunt
   by gritting teeth.
Oh no—not now!
  No sound, no bodily pain
  Can now drown out the
   silent
  Sobbing of my heart.
My wounds bleed only tears
  For my wife shall too soon Die.

It is not death

That bothers me—

It is the timing!

The first few weeks were busy beginning treatment protocols and adjusting to the dreaded diagnosis of inoperable cancer most likely originating in the liver. That this tumor is extremely rare did not ease the shock nor the numbness that comes with the reaction that few options exist.

The first six months were tolerable but not good. The last six month were very bad.

My Footsteps

Fall a different pattern now
  And crowded beaches seem
  As vacuumed spaces.
Time rushes by in uncanny rubber
  Slowness
At times stretching
  seemingly forever
  Only to snap onward
  In jerky swift motion.
I remember too much
  Yet recall is gone
  For things I cherish.
Important things now
  Are the trivia of yesterday.

I am living a lesson of life,
  My friends—
  So look, listen, learn
  All you can.
For I am now living my
  Philosphy of life
  And I am about to become
  Unglued!

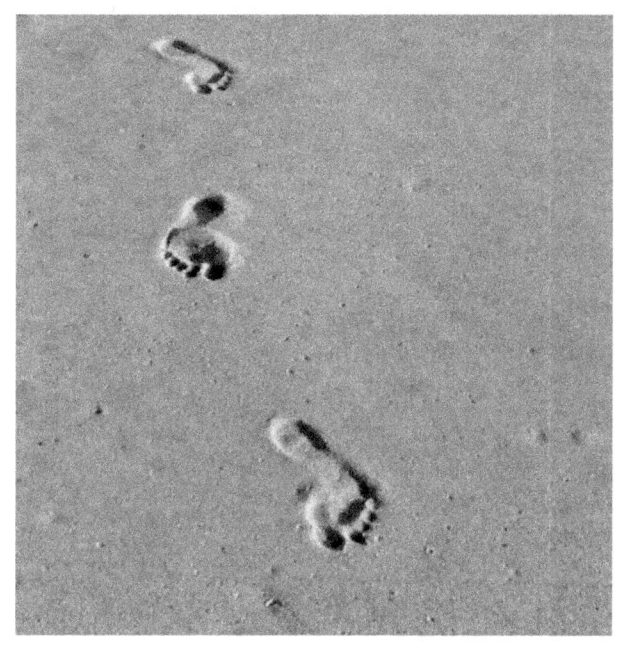

Hope to despair to be repeated over and over is exhausting to both, the sick and the caretakers. I will eventually be depleted of energy reserves.

I watch you from day
to day
  And tread the yo-yo's
     Path of Hope
            to
                  Despair
I tire not of work
  On a horizontal plane
  from day to day
It is the vertical
            Fall
                and
                    Rise
That exhausts me,
  And each rise is a little Less
      than the
            Fall.

I have watched you fall,
  Tremble with weakness,
  Cry a minuscule sigh, and stifle pain.
My stomach bears it all.
  I hide and smile
  Yet I cannot deny
  Your hair that falls
  And stops the shower drain.
Now the slowing of speech,
  The smile
   The gait
    The wit
     The love of us all.
All things of our lives are
  Now consumed by the pain
  And the slow, persistent
   Growing cancer.

My wife was a very remarkable person. She was totally concerned about the care of our children and their welfare after her death. She did not want to die on a holiday as the memory may tarnish the events for the children. She reviewed possible replacement of her in the role of mother. It is incredible that anyone could even consider such topics when given a diagnosis as she had received.

We deny a lot on the surface

  Joke and laugh at times
  Both now the unspeakable
  Know we must speak
  Of dying
Time when physical love
  Can no longer be
Time when children must be
  Weened
These times sneak through
  And practical matters are covered.
How can I survive when
  You are gone!
I cannot remember where
  The pots are
    Or how to correctly mix
    Rice and water.

The fear I have most
Is my loneliness
And the loss of our family's
Memory.
You alone carry
Those silly, vital
Remembrance of children's
Hair, smiles, weights, teeth
What we did
Our closeness.
I just cherished all these in a
Total way—
You itemized the bill.
What will I do?
What will I forget?
What have I forgotten?

True intimacy involves much more than physical expression. It is the freedom to reveal hopes, fears, strengths, weaknesses, needs and desires with complete trust that such revelations would never be used to control nor manipulate. Thus partners can experience complete love and caring, making this journey through life meaningful.

The time is here
And I push hard
With faked passion
Yet love so real
To allow me to continue
Without crying.
The time you feared is here.
For we shall not
Make love again.

I bury myself in
    business
And walk the
    beaches
Alone.

They say living is the art
  Of dying.
Death is part of life.
Are we living more than others?

I do not feel bitter

Our life has been better than most
But I cannot believe
  I needed any lessons of empathy
Nor pain.
Can anyone understand?
 Some try
  Others want to touch pain
  Only to run away to sigh in relief.
Curiosity brings most
 Honesty on our part
  Sends most away.
Some stay
 And stay.
Bless them,
 Bless them!

I wanted and need someone just to hold me and let me be consumed for a short time by my grief and be responsible only to myself.

Touch me,

Touch me,

And feel me human.

I do not believe
 That what is happening
  Is at all unfair,
   As has been stated by others.
Rather, I am awe-struck
 By the total fairness of this life
 That engulfs us all.
That you should die young
 With life just opening before us.
 That pain and sorrow shall
  Come even to me
  Without understanding the why,
Is the essence of fairness.

There was a definite point when I was able to separate myself emotionally from the daily events and accept the inevitable outcome. At this point, I could begin to function in a quasi-organized manner.

October

Good time is gone
 There is no more
  And I am told this is our ending.
The pain
 Oh pain to shatter the
  Children's illusions of
  Eternal joys and founts of
motherhood
  Is done to conclusion.
I turn you loose.
 My love,
  You are now free forever
  And I mourn only for me,
   My Loss
   My emptiness

And hope for your forever.
My wife is no more—
　Love, yes,
　　Cherish, yes,
　But the body is that
　　Of another patient.
I turn you loose!

How important is Touch!

I know too well!

Too well!

Who can understand?

Who can accept
  The freedom I feel?
It changes not my love
  But allows me to think
  In tomorrows again.
I shall live—
  Our children shall live.
  We all shall die
  But after you.
What we were
  And what we shared
  Shall live forever
  And cannot ever be
changed,
  Although there remains
  No tomorrows.

The agony I feel
Is not the fear of
Your being gone.
For you, as you were,
Shall never be again.
All things are changed
No longer to return
Again to our life as it was.
What is agony now
Is the when—or if—
This will be over
And the great uncertainty
This brings.
I am exhausted!
I can bear little more.
Our trip through life is over.
We can never return to Dallas
Or beyond.

I will love you forever
As I love myself
For you and I
Are One.

We had airline tickets to return to North Carolina to see her parents (who had yet to come to visit during her illness) one last time. We were to leave the afternoon of December 22. The night before we were to leave, she again slipped into coma. She did not want to go to the hospital again, so I lay in the bed with her and listened as the breathing changed from normal to that of one near death. I still do not know how I was able to do this, but I knew and respected her wishes

At this point, she was taken once again to the hospital for her last trip.

December 22

You slipped into coma again.
  I feel the ending now.
The event was a struggle,
  Your refusal to leave home
    for what you must have
    Known to be the last time as well,
  Was defiance to what must be.
And fight hard
  You did!
But though respected
  this struggle in futility
    Hurts me
      for I must watch all.
We removed you limp, and

Quiet,
 Except for the too loud,
  Too broken,
   Breathes struggling yet
    Too live.
I am numb.
 I watch as from afar.
  Too tired,
   Too depleted to cry
   Or protest again.
If your aunt were not here,
 We would refuse help
  Beyond the bed
  And the cool cloth for the head.
I cannot demand this now
 And I am sorry.

She remained in a coma through Christmas and into the new year.

On and on this
nightmare marches.
Never ceasing to get a little worse,
Even when worse seems impossible.
This struggle is broken
Only by episodes of uncanny
Snatches of clarity
And you ask to be held.
Yet unaware, it seems
Of nothing more.
You cling to life,
An incredible time,
I believe because of our children.
Yet too small to leave
And our life that was
And is so good
  Together.

An Afterthought

I feel your belly
  Tight and smooth—but hard
And I cannot help remembering
  This feeling when it held life
    Full of hope and joy.
Strokes would bring movement
  And resentful kicks and
  We would laugh at the
    Impatience of an unknown
    Individual yet to be born.
I feel you belly
  But cannot keep my hand
    There to stroke that which
    Will take you from me
    And deliver you only from
      This life—my arms.

January 2nd

I rested in jerky snatches of sleep,
　Somewhere short of full awareness and depth
　When things seem clear
　Yet the body refuses to move.
It's morning now
　And the watch continues
　Preparing me—as it were—
　　For the ending.
I had a dream—
　No, not really so
　For no events occur—
　　Just thoughts
　　When we thought together.
I will be happy—you say.

No, I counted not as happy
As we—together
Yet you insist that I too,
Will be happy yet with another.
How could I be happy—as happy as we—
With someone else?
Then the thoughts seem to clear.
I am now in the state of maturity
We both have sought,
For now each person can be accepted
For what each really is
The strengths and weaknesses of all—
Even ourselves.
No judgments are made
All are happy for what each is.
There is no need to explain nor justify
For what we had or had not

    Stands alone—
    Uncomplicated—
    Unaltered—
    Accepted totally.
I love you.
  I shall always love you
  And what we had is over,
  But shall remain forever.
I am at peace with myself
  And all the world.
The trunk we have is not for your trivia
  As you planned—
  Rather for me
  As the place to keep those items
  For the children
  That were once important to me.
I could rest no more—
  Although the reality of these

thoughts
  With you were pleasant.
  They unnerved me
  And I felt a dichotomy of desire
  To continue and to escape.
I arose from the bed,
  Spoke lightly to those,
  Awaiting with me in heavy gloom,
  When the hospital called to tell me
  That you had died.
I accept what I felt
  For what is was—
    Warmth, love and
completeness,
    Good thoughts and happy memories
    Of sharing our life as it was, to-
gether.
The trunk remained

Until at my leisure
   I examined that which seemed
concrete.
It too, spoke of love, warmth and truth
  As it continued all those little
      important
  Things from you to our children.
Now is the time for life
  And living.
It is over!

After her death, I had to face the unpleasant challenge of trying to please relatives and society to fulfill their expectations of grief and decorum. I wanted a simple wooden coffin; family expected an elaborate metal one. The funeral director essentially demanded a concrete vault to slow deterioration and truly believed that the lining of the coffin should be silk—something she nor I had ever desired. Her mother wanted a large bronze marker to cover the entire grave, while I believed that a year of college would be a more noble remembrance for our children. There was no way I could escape without some castigation, so I made decisions—some good, some bad—and tried to forgive myself.

I believe

Our society views death with
Unreasonable awe.
Although we cannot hold the spirit,
We want to keep the body in perfect
State—
 Forever!
What do we wish?
That someone 2000 years from now
Should view our bodies as some
Mighty king!
I rather believe they would laugh
At the futility of our gesture.
For one cannot obtain immortality
By preserving the body a few more
trivial years.
No concrete vault will stop

The final crumbling, but
A few insignificant years.
Please, let me grow flowers.
Your mother wants a bronze
Slab to cover the entire grave.
What a waste!
Remembrance of importance
Occurs only in the heart
And no metal slab can be
A measure of
Caring.
Love
Caring
Tributes
Should be given through
Touching
While alive.
Metal slabs become monuments

Only to those who sold them
And are testimonies to guilt
Of things unsaid—
Touches withheld.

After Winter Must Come Spring!

February

I am as the struck turtle
  Who now feels the air for hurt
  With nerves, raw and ready
  To flash a return to the shell.
My pace forward, too, seems impeded
And yet I know the neck must extend
  To move forward
  And that each hesitation
  Is a heartbeat lost—forever.
I must keep pace!
  I must not involute!
    I must live again!

It is over!

God, over sounds so permanent
That I feel afraid to ever whisper
 It's over.
Yet, beyond the fear
 Is the new joy
 Just to be able to say
  To myself
It's over!

There is a small corner
    of
My heart that remains happy
Within this darkest segment
  Of my life that grows
    On stolen moments of happiness
    Shared with you.
This corner is slowly strengthening
  Awaiting the spring day
  When it, too, germinates
  Eventually filling my awakening
  To perennial springtimes.

In the bleakest winter of
    my life
You gave me hope for the spring.
As the vestige of last year's shower,
I feel the seepage of the thaw
  Before the flow of the melt.
I now can dream once again
  Of stretching for the sun,
  Basking in its glow
  And singing again to the
    Beauty of this life.
At times the world is as a dark room
Without known shape or form—
A vertiginous maze
  With no reference or beginning point.
How wonderful then is the human

hand
That touches then waits for guiding
gestures,
Never holding unless held,
Releasing on slackening grasp,
Holding tight when sensing fear,
Drawing close when requested.
Thus this nebulous haze is explored
In ever so expanding circles
of confidence
Until a defining ray of light is found.
That moment can be shared
With the joyful acclaim,
Look! The hope we have found!
My friend and I,
In this moment of crisis!

I reached out my hand
Into a darkened world
  And touched yours.
Your touch felt warm and good,
  Becoming the clasp
  That mellowed
  Into the caress.
And my world no longer
  Appears as dark
  Because you make me
  Happy.

Sweet agony
The thorn verifying life
Need finding fulfillment
Love congealed by
Fear of loss
Makes me hold tighter.

People are but the
 Flowing ink
  Amid their dynamic
   histories
  Written through blood
  Or shared time.
Loss is a deletion of
 A portion of one's history
Being lost
 Is having no history!

You Are Gone

My heart feels as hollow
  As the echo of the unseen
  Tram across the meadow.
A heart can hold
  Just so many tears
  Until it ruptures—
  To ink despair across
    Living.
      I miss you so!
The heart never breaks
  From too much love.
It ruptures when empty!

I think of you now
  and it is
  like a soft dream of a child
  with fluffy pillows and clean
  linen with all the smells of
  sweetness that speak of
security
  and love.
I think of you and hold once
again
  your face in my hands and
trace
  the lines of your forehead and eyes,
cheeks and ears—to the warmth
  of your neck.
I feel the textures of your skin,
  smell the fragrance of your hair,

*sense your willingness for my touch
   melt into glowing pleasure.
Your breath tells me how you feel,
   replacing your eyes, now closed,
   as the mirror of inner thought—
   and I kiss your lips.
Softly—so softly—we float
   reaching for the inner being
   of each other into the early
   morning
Has it been so long?*

It is the time of year

When flowers spring
In colored profusion.
Like sunbathers who stretch
Their arms still bleached
from winters darkness
To the sun—
Then tanning into
A rainbow of hues.
And the earth shares the
celebration
Assuming the sweet smells
And dampness of new birth.
All of life seems to share in this
Joyous awakening that is proclaimed
In the songs of the mockingbird
And the return of the martin.

It is the season of change!
  I see it in your face,
  Feel it in my smile,
  Touch it in your hand,
  And speak
    Of Spring.

I walked today
The paths of half
My life ago
In the quiet drizzle
Of North Carolina fall.
I walked these paths and noticed only
The deepening of the ruts beneath
The thousands of feet that followed
mine,
And the washing of the rains.
I longed for you there
And within my awareness
I expected to see you again
And feel the surge of recognition
With the anticipation of the
Caress.
Sweet joys fleeted through my heart

To be shattered by reality
Once more—again.
From the surge of the high
To the depth of my loss
I flutter
 To suppress— once again—
 Feeling I believed conquered.
It is not places—not old familiar
 Setting of park benches, trees,
 Grasses, nor the rain.
These only remind us of what we miss
 Of that which gives things
 And places melancholy power.
Only the people with whom
 We shared these joys.

Life is a Gift

Life's events and memories
  Must be created.
Come
  Share my life
  And mark it's passage
  Through memories
    Together.

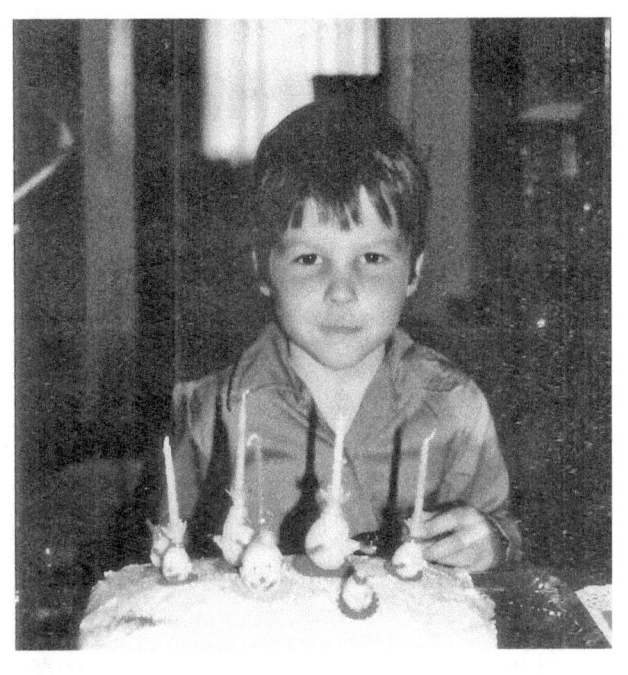

Am I as the child soul,
 free to ride the invisible winds,
  Living to love all I touch,
  Loving the touch all I will?
As the thistledown, I am, too, free,
 Yet bounded by the whims
   Of yet freer winds,
   Balanced in delicate
    suspension,
   To tempting to grip,
   Yet impossible to hold
   Without destroying its inner beauty.
I long for such freedom
 To love and share
 Without possessing nor
 Being possessed.
As the thistledown,

I float in life somewhere
Between the down and the
thistle.
Come touch me.
Allure me with tenderness
For I follow the eddies
Of the graceful stroke
And dwell in the stillness
Of quiet thoughtfulness.
While awaiting my
germination.

Dreams

Like Clouds
Have no schedule
Cannot be held in the hand,
Confined by words, nor
Expected to maintain
Predictable patterns,
But, may appear, disappear
Waiting to reform in another
Place or time
Responding to no command.
Yet without
Dreams or clouds
Would the oak grow?

A falcon lit upon my shoulder.

His firm grasp and piercing eyes
Belying his weight of feathers.
We cupped our hands together
To quench our quest
In the sparkling of stardust.
And time
It dripped in shimmering drops
Through our fingers as we gently
Grasped to hold each dream
We hold the quicksilvered dream
But an instant—then it was gone
Yet it is that which everyone seeks
And seldom finds—
That which neither can be sought
Nor asked to appear.

For who can say
"Falcon come from your freedom
Flight to sit upon my shoulder
Tonight."
And if we could hood those eyes
Or shackle the feet to exclaim
"Look, what is mine to keep—To hold or
let fly at my
Command!'"
Where then would be the sparkle
Of the shimmering eyes
Or the stardust in it's touch?
No! Oh no—it must be by
Choice!
What we have
What we desire
Must come by the magic of free will.

To hope and dream
is to aspire to embrace
the challenging allure
of the impossible
Achieved—
the dream often
becomes the mountain
desent.

Apathy

It begins in softness
  Hardly noticed
  Growing until
  Suddenly you know it is there
  Commanding a corner of your being.
Slowly apathy appears
  As the fog at dew point
  Clouding the vision
  Arousing anxiety at any
  Exuberance of living.
It is not as strong as a death-wish
  Nor as obvious as a
destructive gesture.
  It is the haunting lack of fear that
life

May not go on if the plane should
    fall,
  Or accident occur
  That creeps into my daily existence.
Where is the exuberance that once
  Greeted each day—
The embrace of the earth with all
  Her smells, colors, and textures?
When can I again watch for the flash
  Of green of the sunset
  Or notice the crystal of a cold winter
day;
  Note the purple and browns unique
  To the day's end of autumn
  Or the golds of summer?
I am tired of this cloak—this misty
  Choking shroud that seems to absorb
  Frantic struggles to suffocate

A little more.
Clearing, I know must come from within
　Which is the hardest part.
As for now,
　I have at last felt the soft, velvet
　Fog of apathy;
　Recognized its haze
　And am desperately
　Trying to blow it
　Away.

Wait for me there—
    by the garden gate
And tell me if you hear the robin's song,
  For I have this nagging fear
  That I may have missed the spring.
Wait for me by the gate
  Along this path of life
  And tell me which way
  The swallows fly.
We cannot turn back
  Along the narrow path.
  So is all we can hope is to hear
  The songs; feel the winds
  Of springtime past?
Hold me close
  Kiss me eagerly
  Listen with me

To hear the rush of changing winds
And smell again the sweetness
Of spring flowers' blush.
Hold me close. Awake me again.
My fears will hush
And the seasons will matter less
As you will fill me again with feel-
ings of
Springtime present
Or Springtime past.
I will cling to each awakening sense,
Thrill to each vibration,
So I will never again endure
The nagging insecurity
Of wasted moments past.

The Marsh

The marsh land stands in springtime splendor
Of rice green in irregular patches
Of velvet smoothness that moves in waves
As a negative of the wind
Upon the mirrored smoothness of darker waters.
Ripples in the water dance in synergy with
The velvet grasses whose dance is to
A different cadence.
All move to the harmony of the stronger
Yet subtle commands of the moon and tides.

A desolate place, it exudes starkness with
Nothing to resist the assault of
Wind and tides.
Darkness if character oozes from the floor,
Muddies the waters so each step is
Swallowed in uncertainty.
Classic inhospitality for life on first veiw,
The marsh pulses with new life.
The birds know
  Moving like ice statues, cranes and herons
  Stalk their survival in counter
  Ripples among newborn sea life.
The redwing blackbird surveys
  His grounds as he barks his

Territories from cane to cane.
Crabs and gulls glean the leavings,
  While life passes onward—
  Settling as waste and slime
  Oozing mud, bubbling gases
  Yielding new life—
  New circles.
All is balanced
  Life to death
  Through slime and ooze
Some see beauty only in
  The surface pulses
Few grasp the wonder,
  The awe of it all!
It moves me! The marsh.
  I feel its undulations as my
  Pulse beat
  I see the barren land

Exuding life
As the soul of a friend that slowly
Unfolds as a springtime flower
When confidence grows.
I respect the marsh as the power,
The awesome region
Where life ends
Without regret—
Only to grow more flowers.

Perhaps it was the intense need I felt to re-establish my life or the fact that Lynda selected the person she believed best to replace her as mother of our children, or just my stubbornness to move forward, I fell in love and re-married too soon. The decisions I made were my own for I was advised to wait but I was determined to have again that which I had lost.

Soon, all of my many faults were illuminated and reflected upon on a regular basis. I then began to believe all the incriminations were indeed true and that Lynda was truly a saint to allow me vast latitude without complaint. For five years I withdrew to bury myself in work. Multiple counseling sessions only seemed to verify the defects of my personality. Individual counseling finally helped me believe that "I am not that bad," and I learned of invalidation being a powerful method of control.

For more years than Lynda and I were married, I held to the union mainly for fear of further loss and strong resistance for divorce. But my personality had changed and my view of life was not as vibrant.

Further counseling still presented no resolution and I internalized my anger with what I perceived to be the greatest mistake of my life.

I will always be grateful for the real help stabilizing my family as much as possible, but the anger that grew within, I knew, would shorten my life. One last individual counselor was seen and forever changed my life, validating my worth and giving me strength to move forward. More than invalidation, I then understood the power of withholding approval and affection to manipulate and control.

This was to be a long journey, for I never wanted to be captive again through love and caring. To profess love for anyone was now most difficult for feat of again losing myself. The happiest day of my new life was to say "I love you" without fear nor hesitation.

Truth is as variable as
   perception.

Forgiveness is not only for the forgiven.

Martyrdom is usually it's own
   reward.

Perhaps the greatest sin is to waste a
   life being unhappy when choice
   is available.

Rules are made to keep idiots
   out of trouble—wise men
   to interpret.

There are three special planes plus time.
  Unless one occupies all four,

no experience is completely the same.
So truth is an individual perception
Intrepreted through experience.
No one can invalidate one's truth if
self honestly derived.
Individual truths can be
argued but not invalidated.

When young, I spent the first half of my life defining whom I wanted to be and shared this life.

After loss of my wife, re-marriage and trying to regain that which was lost, I spent the next portion of my life learning what I was not.

From the one who should care, I heard that I did not listen; felt when told I did not care; was shocked to hear all the things I was perceived to be but never desired to become; lived in a house without music where the heart did not sing and clocks did not run.

All these things pushed me to hope again. The last of my life is here. I must define again who I am; whom I wish to be.

I walked the grassy plains
of the Llano uplift among
granite boulders beneath
azure sky, listening to bird
songs and the whisper of the
wind through the grasses and leaves.
Suddenly I exited into a loft
of rocks that displayed an
expanse of green hills split
by the clear blue-green
waters of the Llano River.
The sight was overpowering
and in that moment I raised
my arms to the sky, my
palms open, my head
uplifted as to scoop a
portion of this view into my grasp.

And I thanked God for this sight, the air, the sky, the smells of earth, for this life so full of joy, for love and being loved; for the chance of tomorrow.

At the instant, I knew I was a child of God, loved by God, and within God. I knew as clearly as I saw the sky what He expects of our lives—as simply as the joy one has when one has given another joy.

God's hope for us is to live with joy and thankfulness through adversity and travail, giving and receiving love.

When our hearts are as joyous as mine—God smiles. I love you and through this I have touched the face of God!

Lessons Learned

1 - Enduring loss is a part of the human experience.

2 - Cherish all things in this life for we do not know how long our time lasts.

3 - Pray, meditate, clear the mind of greed, devious or malicious thoughts in order to make good choices.

4 - Once clear decisions are made, proceed forward with the interest of family and friends foremost.

5 - Learn to forgive yourself for choic-

es made as clearly as possible for mistakes and errors will occur.

6 - Take counsel only from those asked.

7 - People will...
a) flee for fear of somehow contracting your problem
b) approach for curiosity
c) few will offer any help possible when asked
d) some will become angry when their counsel is rejected.

8 - Good-hearted people will flood you with materials that promise resolution if only one has enough faith, never realizing that poor outcome may be

unavoidable infers that the affected had inadequate faith. God and life do not function in this manner or there would be many very old, healthy people.

9 - Friends and family who may have guilt over failed closure and good feelings will get angry, usually focused upon the survivor.

10 - Forgiveness is as important as for one's self as for the forgiven.

11 - Forgiveness does not imply re-exposing one's self to bad behavior.

About the Author

J. Thom Love grew up in rural North Carolina. After high school, he attended and graduated from Duke University; followed by earning his medical de-  gree from the University of North Carolina School of Medicine. After obtaining his medical degree, he joined the US Navy, where he completed the Navy School of Aviation Medicine. In the Navy, Thom served on the teaching staff of the US Naval School of Aviation Medicine for two years.

He volunteered for service as a flight surgeon with the 1st Marine Air Wing in Viet Nam. His service in Viet Nam was awarded with the Bronze Star with Combat V, two Air Medals and the South Vietnamese Medal for medical mission to the South Vietnamese people.

Upon return from his service in southeast asia, he completed his surgical training at the Univeristy of Texas and Parkland Hospital in Dallas, Texas. Following his residency, he joined the teaching staff of the Univeristy of Texas Medical School in Galveston, Texas.

In all his endeavors he was supported by his wife, and high school sweetheart, Lynda until her death from cancer in 1975. At the time of her death, she left three children, ages 13, 10 and 6.

Dr. Love has practiced medicine in academic areas, private pracice, and lastly in group practices. He is now remarried, residing in the DFW area, finding the happiness and contentment he believed was lost. Now retired, he completed the writings composed during the time of illness and death of his first wife.

www.ingramcontent.com/pod-product-compliance
Lightning Source LLC
Chambersburg PA
CBHW061641040426
42446CB00010B/1523